Collecting Plastics:
A Handbook and Price Guide

Jan Lindenberger

1469 Morstein Road, West Chester, Pennsylvania 19380

Three piece canister set. Plastic with red floral design, $20-25.

Title page photo:
Clown bank, marked U.S.A. A penny is placed in the
hand, and then goes into the mouth. Celluloid,
$35-40.

Copyright © 1991 by Jan Lindenberger
Library of Congress Catalog Number: 91-65648.

Printed in the United States of America.
ISBN: 0-88740-335-2

Published by Schiffer Publishing, Ltd.
1469 Morstein Road
West Chester, Pennsylvania 19380
Please write for a free catalog.
This book may be purchased from the publisher.
Please include $2.00 postage.
Try your bookstore first.

We are interested in hearing from authors
with book ideas on related subjects.

Contents

Back cover photos:
Top left—Chef holding salt and pepper. Red plastic, $12-15. Top right—Cookie jar. "Aunt Jemima, F & F Co., Dayton, Ohio." $300-375. Bottom left—Clock marked "Kit Cat Klock, Calif." Red plastic with rhinestones. The tail swings, and the eyes go back and forth, $40-48. Center right—Cat and dog salt and pepper marked "F & F, Dayton, Ohio." Plastic, $12-15. Bottom right—Salt and pepper cats marked "U.S.A." Plastic, $8-10.

Red floral pitcher. Plastic, $9-12.

Around the House

Kid's Stuff

Salt & pepper flower pot with roses as the salt & pepper shakers. U.S.A., $5-6.

Acknowledgements

I want to thank everyone who was kind enough to share their collections with me. Special thanks goes to Nina and Richard Bowles for the kindness and patience they showed to me while I was taking photographs at their home and business, The Antique Mall of Lubbock, Lubbock, Texas.

Thanks also goes to:
Antique Market, Denver, Colorado
Antique Specialty Mall, Albuquerque, New Mexico
Antiques/Art/Collectibles, Lubbock, Texas
Antiques Amarillo, Amarillo, Texas
Classic Century Mall, Albuquerque, New Mexico
Country Co-op Mall, Amarillo, Texas
Lakewood Antique Mall, Lakewood, Colorado
Pegasus Antiques, Sante Fe, New Mexico
Reckollections, Denver, Colorado
Route 66 Antique Mall, El Reno, Oklahoma
Second Impressions, Denver, Colorado
Sin Nombre, Madrid, New Mexico
Sixth Street Antique Mall, Amarillo, Texas
Southwestern Antique Mall, Weatherford, Oklahoma
Stage Stop, Denver, Colorado
Stuff Antique and Collectible Mall, Denver, Colorado
Take a Gander, Denver, Colorado
The Treasure Chest, Springfield, Colorado
And to anyone else I may have forgotten, thanks.

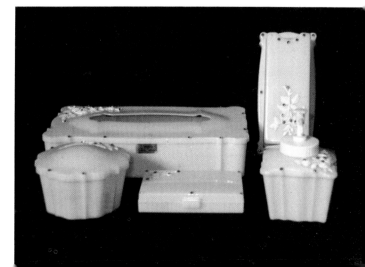

Dresser set marked "Schwarz Bros. Plastics." Yellow plastic, $35-45.

Aunt Jemima doll. Stuffed vinyl, $80-95.

Introduction

It's hard to believe that plastics have become collectible. When you tell someone you're collecting plastics, they tend to raise their eyebrows and look at you like you're totally crazy.

It is not, of course, a new phenomenon. Remember when your grandmother came into your home and wondered why you loved the very same spindle back rocker she always wanted to throw away? What she saw as old and worn, you saw as quaint and beautiful. It is the same with plastics. The world of plastics is interesting and absolutely amazing, and what was once seen as commonplace is now looked at with nostalgia and an eye for its design.

In our modern way of living, plastics have had a tremendous impact. The word plastic, comes from the Greek word "plastikos", meaning "able to be molded or formed into any shape." If you take notice of your surroundings, you will see things made of plastic almost everywhere. As the name implies, plastic is often used because it can be molded into shapes that other materials cannot, which has allowed products and designs to be made that were impossible before. The forms that plastics can take include molding compounds, liquids, adhesives, coatings, solids, foams, laminates, and fibers. Each has its own property and advantage.

Other items were more suitable for plastic than anything else because of the special characteristics it can be given. Things such as jewelry and ink pens use plastic for lightness in weight. Oven proof handles can be made with special formulations that do not melt at high temperatures. Toys and windows are made of plastic for safety reasons. Airplane and car parts as well as radio housings use plastic with special heat resistance qualities. Flooring and counter tops are made in plastic for durability.

On my travels I have found some wonderful plastics. The plastic kitchen items are my favorite,

Three pieces of jewelry. Pink and aqua plastic, $125-150.

especially the colorful bread keepers, wall pockets, salt and pepper sets, creamers and sugars, clocks, and canisters. It sure livens up a kitchen in a hurry when you see that nostalgic bright red canister set or bread box sitting on the counter. These items are still easy to find and are quite affordable, but the number of collectors of kitchen items is just beginning to increase. In another year the prices will rise too.

The plastic items that have been most collectible over the past few years are Bakelite jewelry, Catalin radios, and all realms of celluloid items. Bakelite and Catalin were made from cast phenolics and were used mostly from 1930 to around 1950 when it proved too labor-intensive to be economical. Celluloid, while a wonderful material in many ways, unstable and highly inflammable as it aged. It's very difficult for the collector of these plastics to find a bargain due to their rarity.

Collecting plastics is fun. The colors, shapes, and designs delight the eye and will add to one's personal

Syrup pitcher with flowers on front. Cream colored plastic spout and handle, $18-22.

appearance or to the decor of the home. And in addition it is possible to build a substantial collection without spending a great deal of money...a rarity itself in the world of collecting.

Collecting Plastics: A Handbook and Price Guide is designed for the collector. It can be taken to the flea markets, yard sales, and antique shows and used to evaluate a wide variety of plastic items. The information and photographs on these pages will give the collector an overall understanding of plastics. The price guide, though it reflects the prices in the Mid-West and may differ from other areas, will give the collector a good idea of what an object is worth on the market. (Please note that auction prices will definitely differ from shop prices, and that items will differ in price based on condition and availability.)

I hope you use and enjoy the book, and wish you happy collecting.

Jan Lindenberger,
Colorado Springs, Colorado

A Brief History of Plastics

The first plastic, cellulose nitrate, was produced in 1862 by Alexander Parkes, an English chemist. This chemical was made from the cells in the walls of the plant, cellulose. He found, that by adding camphor, it turned into an ivory like material that could be softened and molded. The product was called Parkesine, after its inventor. Many awards were given him for this product, but it was never in much demand.

Celluloid plastic, a product much like Parkesine, was developed by John Wesley Hyatt in 1868. He began to experiment with collodion, which is a solution of nitrocellulose in ether and alcohol. When exposed to air, it dried into a hard, clear finish. This was used for a finish for wood and metal. Hyatt mixed collodion with camphor and developed celluloid, the first commercially successful plastic. Collars, cuffs, brushes, novelties, dolls, jewelry, toys, billiard balls, vanity sets, shoe horns, are but a few of the items that were made from celluloid in the years that followed.

In 1901 in Germany, Dr. Otto Rohm discovered acrylic plastics. Coal gases, petroleum, air, and water were used to make a clear liquid called methyl methacrylate monomer. This, then, was polymerized into crystal clear, solid plastic. Contemporary trademarks for acrylic plastic include Plexiglass and Lucite. In 1931 acrylic plastics were first used as a bonding agent for safety glass. These are a strong and rigid plastics, and are outstanding for outdoor use. Sunlight or the weather has little or no effect on them. These plastics are used for outdoor signs, auto light covers, contact lenses, windows, and knobs. Because they are odorless and tasteless, they are also used for juice containers and bowls.

In 1909 Dr. Leo Baekeland made an impressive discovery of a synthetic plastic called, phenolic. Also

"Kool-Ade" pitcher. Plastic, $10-14.

known as Bakelite, it was made by a chemical reaction of formaldehyde and phenol. This plastic was excellent for electrical items such as outlets, switches, and auto distributors. It also found use in modern pool balls, telephones, phonograph records, jewelry, toys, and shaver cases.

Cellulose acetate was first developed for commercial use in 1927. Cotton was purified, washed, dried, fluffed, and compressed into bales. These were then treated with acetic acid and acetic anhydride with the aid of a catalyst, such as sulfuric acid. Dyes, lubricants, and plasticizers were then added. When aged and exposed to the ultraviolet rays of the sun, this made a very stable plastic. Lamp shades, lamps, handles, jewelry, toys combs, dresser sets, and auto parts are molded from this plastic.

Aunt Jemima recipe box, marked "Fosta Product, U.S.A." Came in red, green, blue, and yellow. $180-225.

Vinyl resin plastic was first made in the United States in 1928 by the Union Carbide and Carbon Corporation under the trade name of Vinylite. This resin was formed by polymerization of vinyl chloride and vinyl acetate. It was used for phonograph records, can linings, electrical insulation, rainwear, air-inflatable items, and food packaging.

Urea-Formaldehyde plastics first appeared on the market in 1929. With the introduction of this resinous compound, it became possible to make plastic in many bright and beautiful colors.

In 1936 more vinyls were developed. These were tough materials which wore well, and were easily embossed and printed. These new vinyls were used for floor covering, rain coats, upholstery, and shower curtains.

Nylon was invented in 1938. It was tough and resilient, with tremendous strength and a low coefficiency of friction. These qualities made it an ideal material for bearings, fishing line, gears, bristles for brushes, and hundreds of other uses for industry, the home, and in clothing.

Other important developments in plastic technology include:

1938 **Styrenes**. Styrenes are transparent and good at low temperatures. They are commonly used for refrigerator surfaces, food bins, and wall tile.

1939 **Aminos**. Hard and able to be produced in beautiful colors, aminos were used for buttons, dishes, lamp shades, and colored telephones.

1940 **Silicones**. Silicone plastics are heat resistant, and almost like rubber. They are used for sealants in tubs, artificial heart valves, and have many uses as lubricants.

1942 **Polyesters**. When combined with glass fibers, polyesters have the strength needed for use in boats, suitcases, sleds, walls, and auto bodies.

1942 **Polyethylene**. These soft, flexible plastics are not harmed by food or water. They are used for toys, wire insulation, packaging film, and squeeze bottles.

1943 **Fluorocarbons**. The fact that fluorocarbons are unaffected by chemicals and are nearly frictionless, make them well-suited for such common uses as non-stick frying pans, valve seats, and bearings.

1947 **Epoxies**. Because of their adhesion qualities epoxies are widely used in glue, coatings for roads, and floors.

1957 **Polypropylene**. Its break resistant quality makes polypropylene a good material for industrial moldings, ice cube trays, squeezable bottles, and plastic bags.

1962 **Phenoxy**. This is an engineering plastic that is rigid and hard. Phenoxy is used for parts for computers, bottles, drug containers, and appliance housings.

1962 **Polyallomer**. Its high flexibility and long life make polyallomer a good material for hinges. It can be colored and processed easily for uses like hinged cases, notebook binders, and containers.

Since 1962 the plastic industry has been in full force, with new types of and uses for plastic being developed almost daily. Today the packaging industry is the largest market for plastics, followed by the construction industry. Third largest is the electrical/electronics industry, transportation is fourth, and furniture fifth. Other large users of plastics include the appliance industry in sixth place and the toy industry in seventh.

This list makes it clear how far reaching and great the impact of plastic is on our lives.

Plastics in the Kitchen

Bar Ware

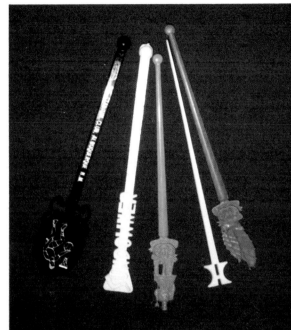

Figural drink stirrers. Plastic, $1.50-2.50

Five piece bar set. Green Bakelite, $38-42.

"Stanley Home Products" shaker. Red plastic, $8-12.

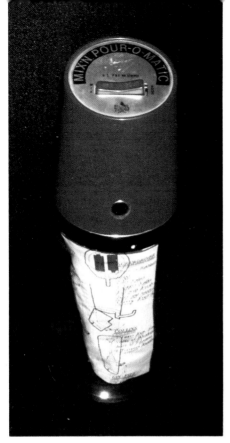

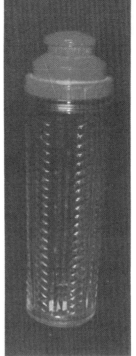

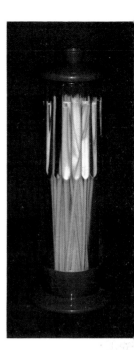

Cocktail shaker marked "Med Co., N.Y." 12½" tall. Glass jar with red plastic top, $20-25.

Clear straw holder with blue top and bottom, $12-16.

"Mix & Pour-O-Matic" cocktail shaker, 10" tall. Glass jar with red plastic lid, $22-25.

Glass seltzer bottle with red plastic spout and trim. Marked "Sparklets Corp., N.Y.," $18-22.

Soda bottle marked "Sparklets Corp., Made in N.Y." 13" tall. Bakelite handle, $28-35.

15

Ice bucket. Aluminum with plastic handle and knob, $10-14.

"Penguin" hot and cold server. Brown Bakelite handles and knob, $18-24.

Opposite page:
Straw holder. 9" tall. Red plastic, unmarked, $16-20.

Ice bucket. Aluminum with Bakelite handles and knob, $12-14.

"Coca-Cola" Cooler. Red plastic outer cover with Bakelite handles, $345-450.

Bowls

Speckled bowl marked "Texas Ware." Grey plastic, $15-20.

Speckled bowl marked ''Texas Ware.'' Orange plastic, $22-28.

Bread Boxes

Bread box, unmarked. Red plastic, $25-30.

Bread box marked "Lusterware Ohio." Aqua plastic, $25-30.

"Lusterware" bread box. Red and white plastic, $25-30.

Bread keeper marked "Burroughs Mfg. Corp." Aqua plastic. $14-18.

Bread keeper, marked "Burroughs Co." Aqua plastic, $14-18.

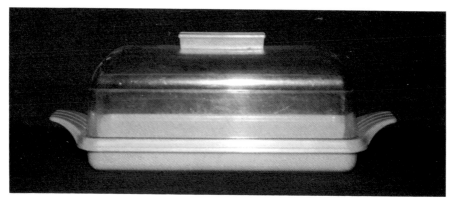

Bread keeper marked "U.S.A." Yellow plastic with a clear cover, $22-26.

Butter Keepers

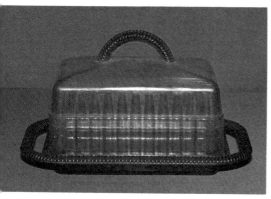

Butter dish with gold bottom and clear top, marked "Plasmetl." Plastic, $12-15.

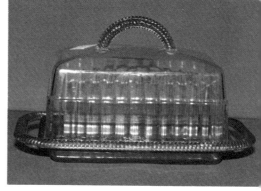

Butter dish. Green bottom with a clear top. The advertising reads "John Deere Farm Equip. U.S.A." $12-15.

Electric butter keeper with a plastic case, $35-45.

Cake Keepers

Cake keeper. White bottom with green cover. Plastic, $18-22.

Cake keeper. Aqua base with a clear cover. Plastic, $15-20.

Canisters

Four piece round canister set. Aqua, pink, yellow, and red plastic, $25-35.

Canister set (sugar missing). Red plastic, $20-25.

Canister set marked "Lusterware Ohio." Aqua plastic, $28-35.

Canister set of red plastic, $25-30.

Four piece canister set. Red plastic, $25-30.

Canister set with flour missing. Yellow with aqua knobs. Plastic.
As is, $8-12.

Canister set (tea missing). Plastic. As is, $10-15.

Children's Dishes

Elf child's cup marked U.S.A. Plastic, $4-6.

Child's Cup marked "Pebbles, U.S.A." Plastic, $4-6.

Milk pitcher and cup marked "Aladdin, U.S.A." Yellow plastic, $85-100.

Mickey & Minnie child's drinking cups. Plastic, $4.50-6.

Child's bowl."Bugs Bunny, U.S.A." Plastic,$4.50-6.

Child's cup marked "Bugs Bunny, U.S.A." Plastic, $4-6.

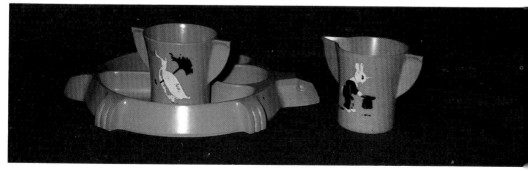

Plastic child's cup and dish by the Richardson Co., Melrose Park, Illinois. It came in pink, blue, and yellow. Marked "Richelain," $6-8.

Child's cup with a handle shaped like the end of a gun, marked "E-Z-Pour Corp." Red plastic, $9-12.

Penguin child's cup. Plastic, $4-6.

Child's cup marked "Campbell Soup Co. West Bend Thermal." $9-12.

Baby dish marked "Baby World Co." Pink with floating plastic animals. $22-25.

"Cream Of Wheat" child's cup. $12-15.

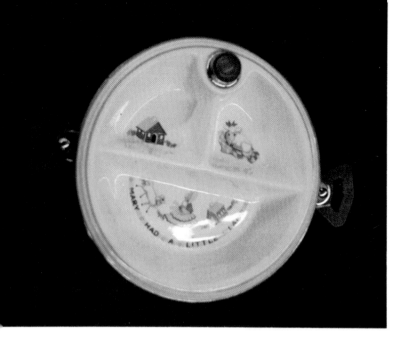

Baby dish with glass insert and
Bakelite handles, $35-40.

"Campbell Soup Kid" child's cup.
Plastic, $6-8.

Baby dish. Yellow Bakelite
handles and plastic insert,
$18-25.

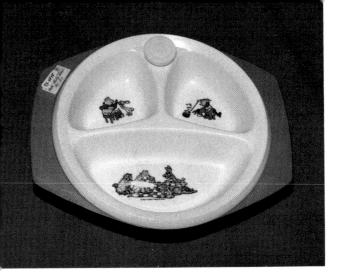

Yellow baby dish with white insert. Plastic, $15-20.

Cookie Cutters

Cookie cutter marked "U.S.A." Red plastic, $3-4.

Cookie molds marked "Sandre & Co., Los Angeles." Plastic, $16-20.

"Bisquick's Bonny Ware" cookie cutter. Aqua plastic, $4-6.

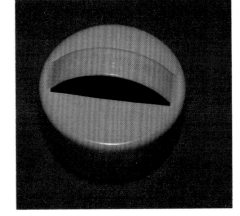

"Popeil" Donut Maker. Red and White. Plastic, $10-14.

Cookie Jars

Santa cookie jar. Marked "Empire, U.S.A." Plastic, $40-45.

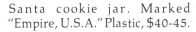

Aqua cookie canister marked "Burroughs Mfg. Co. Los Angeles Ca." Plastic, $18-22.

Cookie jar marked "Aunt Jemima's Cookies." Plastic, $180-225.

"Aladdin Paddy's Pig" cookie jar. Plastic, $35-40.

Cookie jar, marked "Burroughs Mfg.Co." Red and white plastic, $15-22

Cream and Sugar

Cream and sugar marked "Federal Tool Corp." Plastic, $12-14.

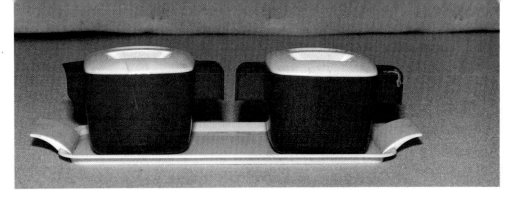

Cream and sugar marked "Federal Tool Corp., Chicago." Red with white lids, white tray. Plastic, $16-20.

Dog and cat cream & sugar, marked "F&F Co. Dayton, Ohio. $12-18.

Canned milk opener and server. As the lid comes down it punctures the can. Plastic, $18-25.

Cow creamer marked "Whirley Indus. Warren, Pa." $4-6.

Aunt Jemima and Uncle Mose cream and sugar marked "F & F, Dayton, Ohio." Plastic, $85-100.

7" sugar jar marked "Measuring Devise Corp., N.Y." Glass jar with plastic spout, $9-12.

Fruit and Salad

Salad tongs. Yellow plastic, $4-6.

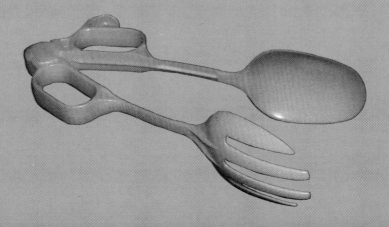

Salad bowl, with tongs, marked "D & D Co." Aqua plastic, $8-12.

Front: fruit dish. Resin and gold swirls, $15-20. Rear: candy server, $10-15. Fruit with plastic beads. 7 pieces, $20-25.

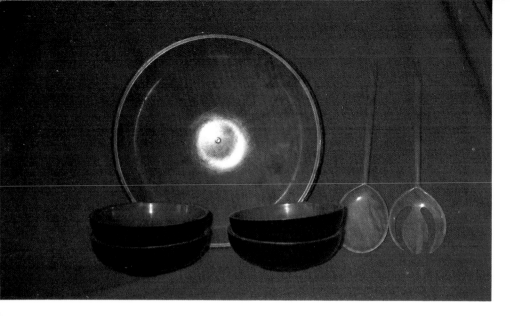

Seven piece salad bowl set, marked "Jardon Thermo." Yellow on black plastic, $45-55.

Kitchen Gadgets

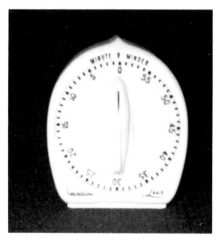

Minute Minder stove timer by Lux. It came in red, yellow, white, blue, $10-14.

Kitchen utensil holder. Red and cream plastic, $9-12.

Drainer, marked "Cook's Grip, Pan Drainer." Aqua plastic, $4-6.

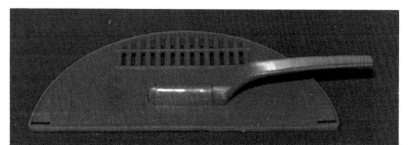

Match holder. Red plastic, $5-8.

Match holder advertising the "Counter Insurance Co." Pink plastic, $8-12.

"Sure Set" liquid thermometer. Red and yellow plastic, $8-10.

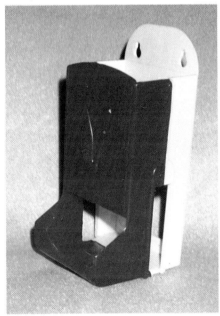

Match holder. Red and white plastic, $12-15.

Red woodpecker tooth pick dispenser with rhinestone eye, on a white log. Plastic, $12-15.

Canned milk holder, marked "Carnation." The lid punches the hole in the can. Red and white plastic, $10-14.

Stainless steel electric tea pot. Bakelite handles and knob on lid, $49-60.

Coffee warmer marked "Vaculator Hill Shaw Co., Chic. Ill." Black Bakelite base and handle, $28-35.

Electric wiener roaster marked "Kiggie." Red plastic, $45-50.

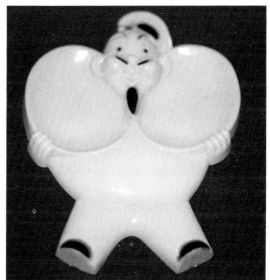

Spoon rest with advertising for Surefine Foods. Marked "Admiration Plastics," $6-9.

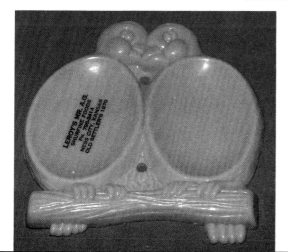

Spoon rest marked "Japan." Pink plastic, $4-10.

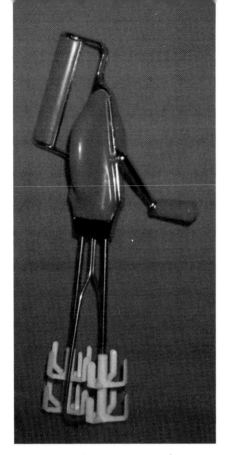

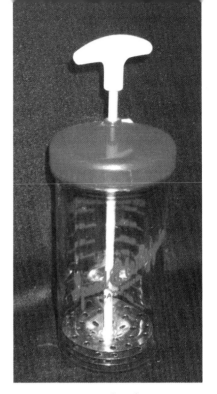

Measuring and whipping jar, marked "Speed & Whipper, U.S.A." Glass jar with red plastic top and two cups, $18-20.
Vegetable brush with red plastic handle, $5-6.

"Maynard" rotary egg beater. Red handle with white whippers. Plastic, $12-14.

Egg whipper marked "The Genuine One Hand Wit Whip, Guaranteed Forever,"$6-8.

Chef radish slicer. Red plastic, $6-8.

Vegetable peeler. Red plastic, $6-9.

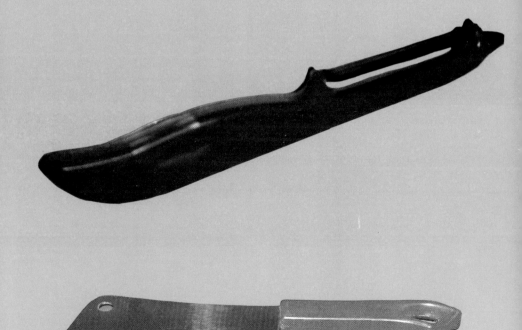

Meat cleaver with red handle. Plastic, $10-12.

Orange and grapefruit peeler. Red plastic, $5-8.

Shredder/Slicer marked "Popeil Bros. Chic. Ill." White plastic, $8-12.

Cheese slicer marked "The Broomfield Slicer." Red plastic, $4-6.

Cheese slicer with a green plastic roller. $4-5.

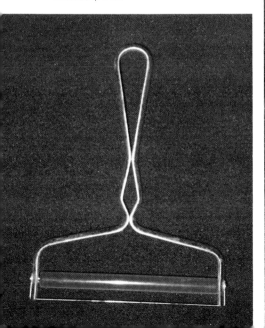

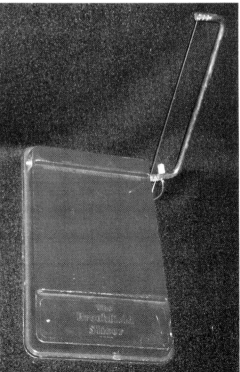

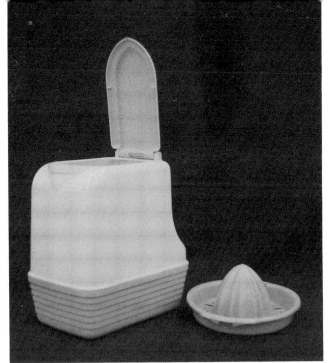

Juicer with a red top and white bottom. Plastic, $8-10.

Pitcher and juicer by Lusterware, U.S.A. Yellow plastic. Pitcher, $12-15. Juicer, $6-8.

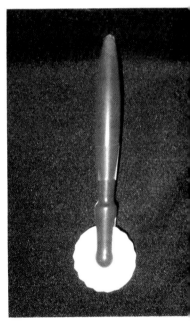

Pie crimper. Red plastic, $5-8.

Red plastic juicer with white plastic insert, $8-10.

Juicer marked "Lustro Ware, U.S.A." Red plastic, $5-8.

Pie slicer. Red plastic,
#8-12.

Egg separator with
advertising for
"Evalona Diary."
$5-7.

Egg slicer, unmarked. Red
plastic, $4-6.

Egg Separator. Green plastic,
$4-6.

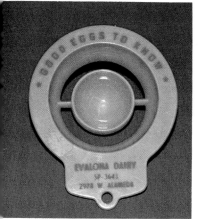

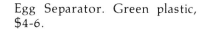

Flour sifter marked "Popeil Bros. U.S.A." White and red handle. Plastic, $5-7.

Flour sifter marked "Bromwells Super-Fine Flour Sifter." Red plastic, $9-14.

Ice cream scoop marked "Lloyd Disher Co, Decatur, Ill." Red with white handle, $12-15.

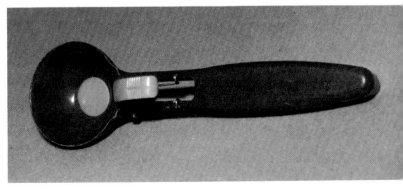

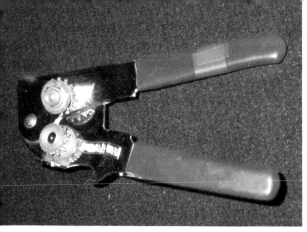

"Swing A Way" can opener. Red plastic, $6-9.

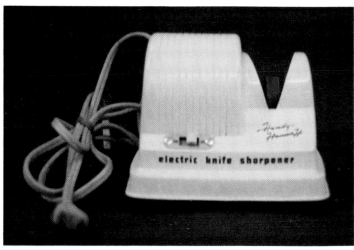

"Handy Hannah" electric knife sharpener by Standard Products Corporation. Bakelite case, $22-35.

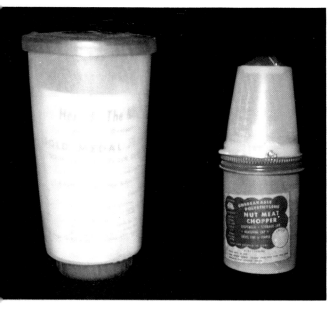

Gold Medal Flour plastic measure and shaker, with removable top and bottom, $18-22. Plastic meat chopper, $12-15.

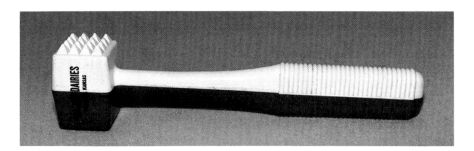

Meat pounder marked "Tip-Top Dairies, Hillsboro, Kansas." Plastic, $15-22.

Ice crusher marked "Dazey, St. Louis, Mo." Plastic bottom, $18-22.

Spice grater marked "Lillo, Italy." Red and cream plastic, $35-40.

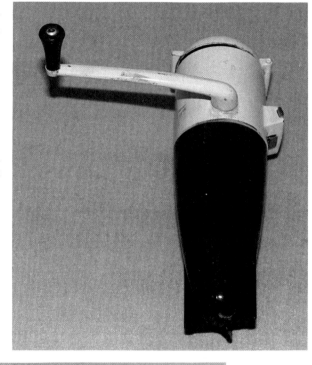

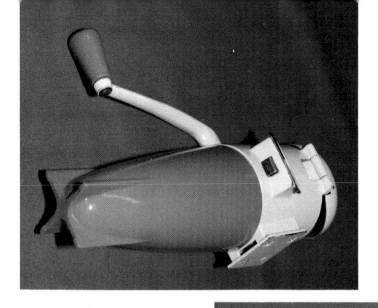

Ice crusher. Green plastic
bottom, $18-22.

Crumb sweeper. Plastic with
red floral design, $9-12.

Measures

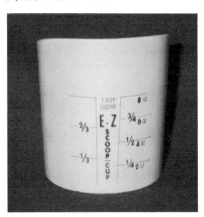

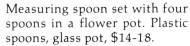

"E-Z Scoop" measuring cup
marked "Advertising Slogan"
on bottom. Yellow plastic,
$3.50-4.50.

Measuring spoon set with four
spoons in a flower pot. Plastic
spoons, glass pot, $14-18.

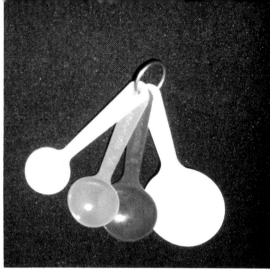

Measuring spoons. Red plastic, unmarked. $4-6.

Set of four measuring spoons, unmarked. Plastic, $5-7.

Yellow measuring spoons marked "Emco U.S.A." Plastic, $4-6. Blue instant coffee scoop marked "Fuller Brush Co.," $5-7.

Measuring scoops. The round ones are marked "Maryland Club Coffee." The pointed one is marked "Folgers." Plastic, $4-6.

Memos and Shopping Reminders

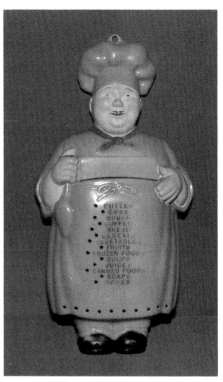

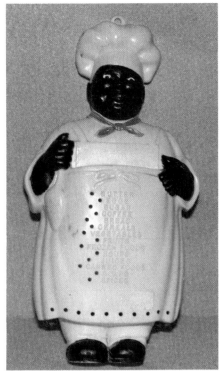

"Noma Happy Chef" shopping reminder. Yellow plastic, $15-20.

Chef memo pad marked "Japan." Plastic, $40-50.

Napkin and Towel Holders

Opposite page bottom left: "Noma Happy Chef" shopping reminder. White plastic, $15-20. Opposite page bottom right: Mammy memo pad marked "Japan." Plastic, $35-45.

Chef napkin holder. Red plastic, $8-10.

Napkin holders. Red plastic baker, unmarked, $10-14. Hummingbirds, $12-15.

Towel holder marked "Onliwon Household Towels." Red plastic, $8-12.

Paper towel holder marked "Scott Towels." Red plastic, $4-6.

Napkin holder. Pink plastic, $10-14.

Wall-mounted dog's head dish towel holder. The towel clips into the dog's mouth. Red plastic, $10-12

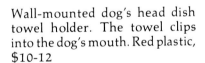

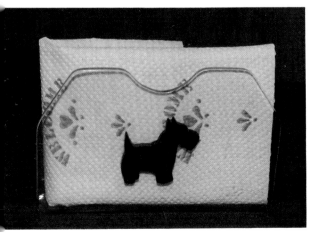

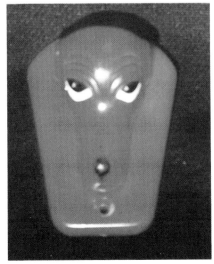

Clear plastic napkin holder, with Scotty dog on front, $7-12.

Lustre-Ware paper towel holder, marked "Columbus Plastic Co., Ohio." Red, $22-28.

Pitchers

Wall hung napkin holder. Pink plastic, $22-25.

Pitcher marked "Blisscraft of Hollywood." Red plastic, $6-8.

Pitcher marked "Beacon, U.S.A." Red plastic, $4-6.

Pitcher. Clear top and yellow
bottom, $10-14.

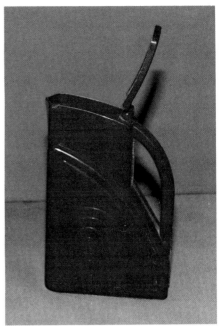

Pitcher marked "Calif. Moulders,
Los Angeles." Red plastic,
$12-15.

Pitcher marked "Burroughs."
Yellow plastic, $10-12.

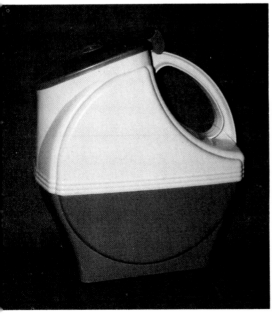

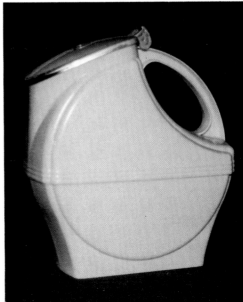

Water pitcher, unmarked. Aqua
and white plastic, $12-$15.

Red plastic milk or water pitcher, $15-18.

Insulated water/juice pitcher. Grey and white plastic, $9-14.

Water or milk pitcher. Green plastic, $12-14.

Refrigerator Pieces

Celery crisper. Clear plastic with celery decor on the front, $18-22.

"King Tappers" bottle cappers. Red, yellow, and blue plastic, $7-10.

Ice cube trays. Red plastic, unmarked. $3-5.

One gallon refrigerator container. Clear plastic. $18-22

Refrigerator container marked "Lusterware, Col., Ohio." Red. $7-10.

Salts and Peppers

Sugar, salt and pepper set marked "Davis Products Co., Brooklyn, N.Y." Red and black plastic, $10-14.

Stove set with salt, pepper, and sugar, marked "Plastic Novelties Calif." Yellow plastic, $24.

Woodpeckers salt and pepper set. Red and gold plastic, $12-15.

Salt and pepper. Red and cream plastic, $4-6.

Aunt Jemima and Uncle Mose salt and pepper marked "F & F, Dayton, Ohio." Large set, $50-65.

Aunt Jemima and Uncle Mose salt and pepper marked "F & F, Dayton, Ohio." Small set, $35-45.

T.V. knobs come out as the salt & pepper, $10.00-12.00. Salt & pepper set marked Carvanite, by Tennessee Eastman Corp., $12-14.

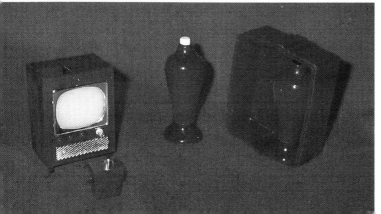

Salt and pepper set featuring Mr. & Mrs. Santa on a tray. Made in Hong Kong, $4-6. Glass strawberries on plastic vine holder. Marked Hong Kong, $3-4. Set of plastic salt & peppers in the form of irons. Marked U.S.A., $5-7.

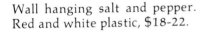

Wall hanging salt and pepper. Red and white plastic, $18-22.

Salt, pepper, and spice containers. Red plastic, $8-10

Salt and pepper marked "U.S.A." Red and black plastic, $4-6.

Salt & pepper boat set, $5.00-6.00. Clear glass salt & pepper set in plastic holder. Marked "Lapin" U.S.A., $5-6.

Butter dish, salt, and pepper. Yellow plastic. Clear top on butter dish. $4-5 each.

Six piece "Royal" hostess salad set from Life Magazine. Black plastic with gold trim, $17.50-22.

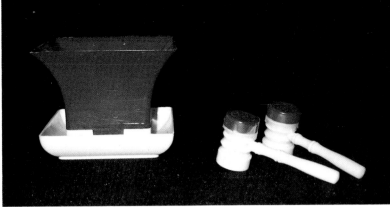

Planter marked "Quality Moulding Co.," Chicago, Illinois, $10-12. Mallet salt and pepper shakers, red and white, $10-12.

Salt and pepper cows marked "J.D.'s, N.Y." Plastic, $8-10.

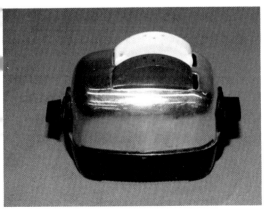

Toaster with toast salt and peppers. Plastic, $10-14.

Magnetic holder holding acorn salt and pepper. Plastic, $10-14.

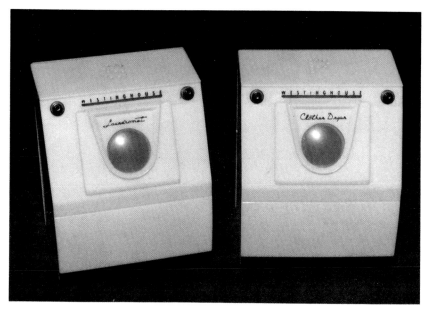

"Westinghouse" washer and dryer, salt and pepper. White plastic, $25-30.

Salt and pepper. Yellow and Aqua Bakelite, $12-15.

Stove set including salt, pepper, and sugar marked "Plastic Novelty Co." Red plastic, $18-22.

Candelabra with candle
salt and pepper. Plastic,
$7-10.

Salt, pepper, toothpick
holder. Green celluloid,
$15-18.

Salt and pepper. Red Bakelite,
$12-16.

Salt and pepper mallets. Red and
blue plastic, $6-8.

Egg-shaped salt and pepper on stand. Aqua plastic, $8-10.

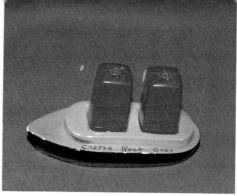

Boat holding salt and pepper. Red plastic, $4-6.

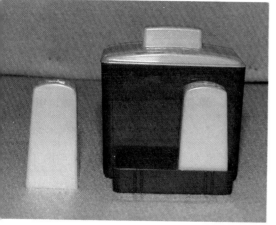

Salt, pepper, and sugar. Red and yellow shakers and lid. Plastic, $8-10.

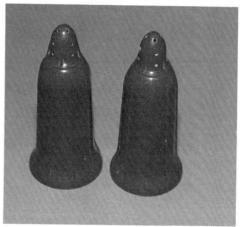

Salt and pepper marked "Hemco Ware." Plastic, $8-10.

Ship with salt and pepper stacks. Red and white plastic, $5-8.

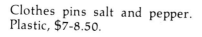

Clothes pins salt and pepper. Plastic, $7-8.50.

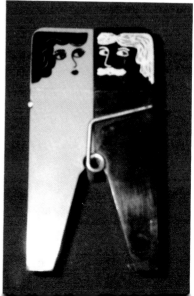

Camel with humps as the salt and pepper. Celluloid, $18-22.

Wall hanging salt and pepper, marked "Superlon,Chic.Il." Red plastic, $18-22.

Sprinkling cans salt and pepper. Clear plastic, $6-8.

Salt and pepper umbrellas. Red and black plastic, $10-12.

Bullet shaped salt and pepper marked "Lapin, U.S.A." Plastic, $5-7.

Salt and pepper. Red and clear Lucite, $4-6.

Serving Pieces

"Kob Knobs" corn cob holders. Green Bakelite handles, $15-20.

Corn Servers marked "Serv-rite, Royal Pacific Co." Yellow and green plastic, $12-18.

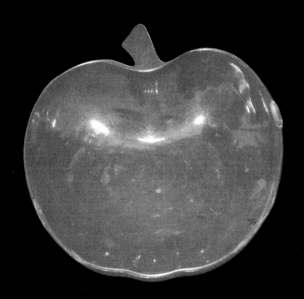

Apple shaped candy dish, marked "A Rogers Product." Red plastic, $3-5.

Pie server. Yellow and green Bakelite handle, $6-8.

Four piece "Hamboware" condiment set. Plastic, $5-8.

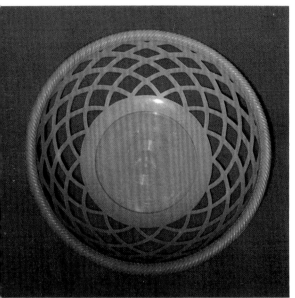

Bread basket marked "U.S.A."
Aqua plastic, $6-8.

Hors d'oeuvres picks in holder.
Red and white plastic, $12-15.

Condiment set with spoons.
Glass jars with yellow plastic
holder and lids, $18-22.

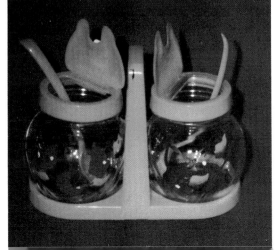

Cracker holder. Silver plastic, $5-7.

Five piece condiment set. Green and white plastic, $12-15.

Egg plate. Red plastic, $5-7.

Spatulas

Red spatula with white handle. Plastic, $8-10.

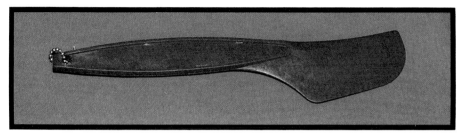

Scraper marked "Yates Dairy." Red plastic, $4-6.

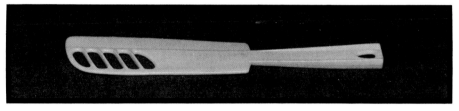

Whip & scraper, marked U.S.A. Pink plastic, $3-5.

Spices

Spice set, marked "Aunt Jemima, F & F Co. Dayton, Ohio."
Three pieces are missing, ginger, allspice, cloves, $35-40 each.

Spice rack. Pink plastic, $24-30.

A red spice rack made to hold the spices from the Aunt Jemima and Uncle Mose set. Plastic, $110-125.

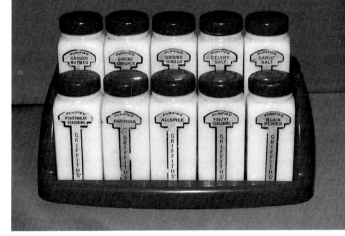

Spice set marked "Griffiths." Glass jars, red plastic lids and holder, $22-25.

Syrups

Syrup or sugar pitchers. Glass bottles with plastic tops. Red, yellow, and white, $4-7.

Glass syrup jar with red plastic
handle. $4-6.

Syrup pitcher with flower
decorated glass jar and yellow
plastic handle, $16-20.

"Sambo Restaurants" syrup
server. Yellow plastic handle,
$185-245.

Syrup pitcher marked "Aunt
Jemima, F & F Co., Dayton,
Ohio." Plastic, $40-45.

Glass syrup pitcher with aqua plastic spout and handle, $8-12.

Syrup pitcher. Glass jar with plastic handle, $4-7.

Tableware

Set of six napkin rings. Red plastic, $5-7.

Candle holders marked "U.S.A." Red plastic, $6-10 for the pair.

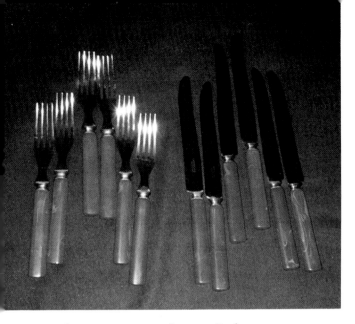

Silverware service for six. Red
handles of Bakelite, $75-85.

Silverware tray. Pink flecked
plastic, $6-8.

Silverware set of six. Yellow Bakelite handles. $75-85.

Six piece "Landers" silverware set. Green Bakelite handles, $45-60.

Pre-war plastic silverware tray, marked "Kampa Mfg. Co." Red, $7-9.

Silverware tray. Red plastic, $6-8.

Set of four glass holders, with coasters marked "Coasterette." Red, yellow, green, and blue plastic, $10-14.

Picnic set, service for four, marked "Flex Ware Calif." Red, green, yellow, and blue, $30-40.

Cup, bowl, and glasses. Aqua, yellow, and pink plastic, $4-6.

Insulated sherbet cups, 3¾" tall. Pink plastic, $4-5.

Handle for a glass. Red plastic, $6-9.

Aqua, yellow, and pink cups with insulated inserts. Marked "U.S.A." Plastic, $2-3.

Set of eight coasters, marked "U.S.A." Pink and aqua, $4-6.

Coaster/nut set. Red, green, and orange plastic, $12-18.

Wall Hangings and Pockets

Wall placque with chef cut out. Black plastic, $4.50-6.

Pink wall pocket marked "Plastic Products, Hollywood, Calif." $10-14.

Wall pocket marked "Plastic Products, Hollywood Calif." Blue, $10-14.

Rooster wall plaque. Red plastic, $4-6.

Wall pocket marked "Plastic Products, Hollywood, Calif." Red plastic, $10-14.

Yellow wall pocket marked "Plastic Products, Hollywood, Calif." $10-14

Dog wall pocket, marked "F&F Co. Dayton, Ohio." Plastic, $12-16.

77

Wall planters. Red plastic, $18-22 pair.

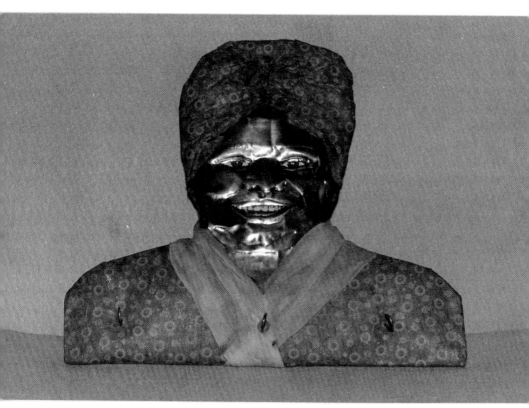

Mammy wall hanger for pot holders. Copper face and vinyl dress, $165-195.

Around the House

"Mastercrafters" clock. The man pulls the cord, and the bell rings." Plastic, $35-42.

"Seth Thomas" clock. Clear Lucite, $45-50.

Kitchen clock. The cat's tail wags, and its eyes move back and forth. Plastic, $45-50.

General Electric kitchen clock. Yellow plastic, $19-24.

Clock with red plastic case and white insert, $12-15.

Owl clock (tail feather missing) marked "Calif. Clock Co." The eyes and tail go back and forth with the movement. Plastic, $18-25.

"Telechron" clock. Red Catalin, $50-65.

General Electric kitchen clock.
Red and white plastic, $19-25.

Furnishings and Decor

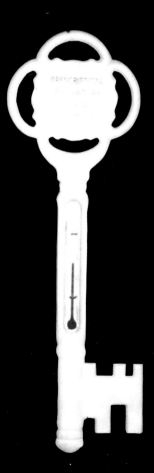

Ottoman with red plastic cover,
$35-45.

Advertising thermometer. Pink
plastic, $4.50-6

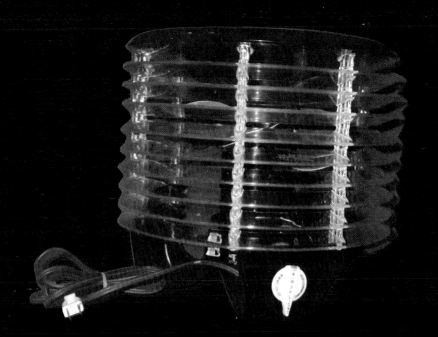

"Air Flight" electric fan. Black plastic, $125–150.

Occasional chair. Aqua plastic, $25–30.

Dog lead puller. White plastic, $6.00.

Floral curtain pulls. Ivory plastic, $6.00 pair.

A lamp from a T.V. sales promotion featuring the green "Metro Ware Plastic Shade." $75.00.

Table and chairs. Chrome and plastic, $300-375.

Kitchen set. Table and chairs, and cabinet/cupboard. Yellow
plastic and chrome. $450-550.

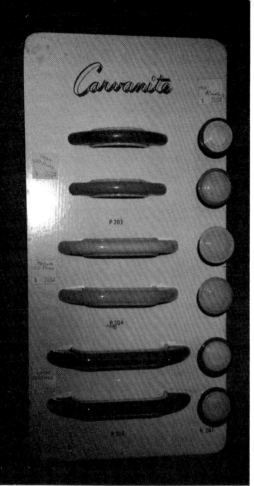

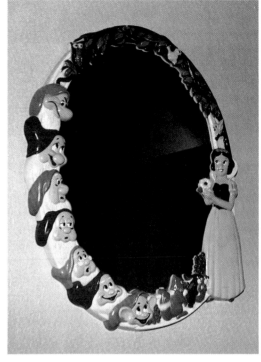

"Snow White & The 7 Dwarfs" mirror. Plastic, $30-45.

6000 sets of "Carvanite" handles for drawers were found in a warehouse. $1.50-2.50 each.

Penguin electric lamp. Pink and blue plastic, $25-30.

Door knocker marked "Amsonfurtsch Corp." Bakelite, $18-25.

Set of five blind pulls in the form of Mammys in polka dot dresses. Plastic, $45-55.

Curtain pin-back, figure in polka dot dress. Plastic, $12-15.

Jewelry

Brown celluloid belt with elephants as the buckle. $20-25.

Red Bakelite hair ornament, $35-40.

Red owl pin. Celluloid, $18-22.

Green Bakelite necklace, $40-45.

Red Bakelite pendant, $22-28.

Pin with shell flowers and bakelite leaves, $8-10.

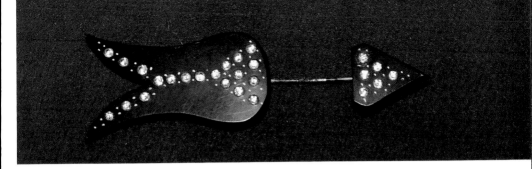

Pin. Black Bakelite with rhinestones, $18-22.

Belt buckle. Cream colored Bakelite, $30-35.

Pin. Green Bakelite, $30-36.

Pin. Green Bakelite, $40-45.

White Scotty dog pin. Bakelite, $10-14.

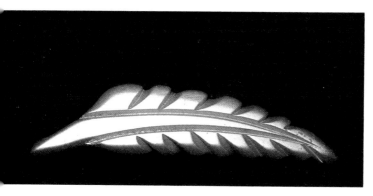

Yellow leaf pin. Bakelite, $18-22.

Green bust pin. Bakelite, $20-25.

Pin with half circles. Pink and blue celluloid, $7-9.

Grey apple pin. Celluloid, $10-14.

Jewelry box. Green Lucite, $35-40.

Pin. Green Bakelite, $40-45.

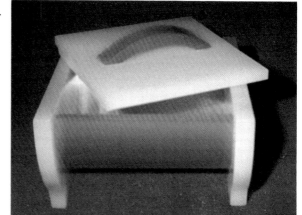

Purse with metal frame, and Lucite top and handle, $35-40.

Laundry Aids

Steam flat iron marked ''Betty Crocker Way.'' Black plastic handle, $22-26.

''General Electric'' iron. Red Bakelite handle, $22-28.

Steam and dry iron marked "General Mills." Black plastic handle, $18-22.

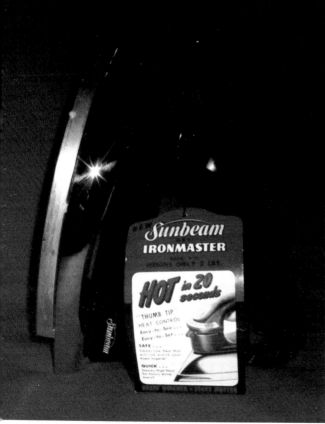

"Sunbeam" steam and dry iron. Bakelite handle, $25-30.

Clothes sprinkler marked "Gotham Ware, U.S.A. Red and white plastic, $12-15.

Clear clothes sprinkler bottle with red top and bottom. Marked "Lustro Ware," $5-8.

Clothesline, marked "Lustro Ware." Red plastic, $12-18.

Pair of clothes sprinklers marked "U.S.A. Plastic." Bottle, $8-12. Lady, $12-14.

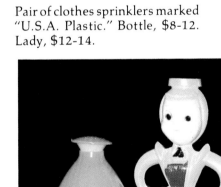

Lady clothes sprinkler. Aqua, red, yellow, and pink plastic, $10-12.

Glove dryers by "Handiforms, N.Y." Pink plastic, $18-22.

Miscellaneous

Yellow Bakelite lock and key, $10-14.

Scouring container with cameo on front. Red plastic, $18-22.

Soap dish, marked "Lustro Ware, Plastic Prod.Inc.," $3-5.

Swan car hood ornament. Stainless steel with Lucite red wings, $15-22.

Fly swatter, marked "Vernon Co., Newton Iowa." Advertising on the handles for the "Alto Creamery." Aqua plastic, $2.50-3.50.

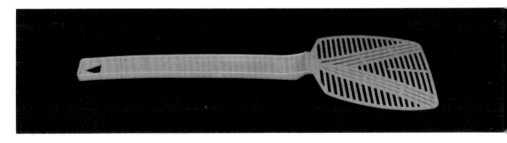

Office

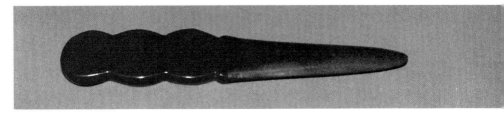

Letter opener. Red plastic, $10-14.

Calendar marked "Plastic Calendar Co. Louisville, Ky." The holder is made of red plastic, $6-8.

Personal Care and Grooming

Shaving set marked "Stanlite U.S.A." Red plastic, $24-30.

Mirror on stand, unmarked. Red and white plastic. $8-10.

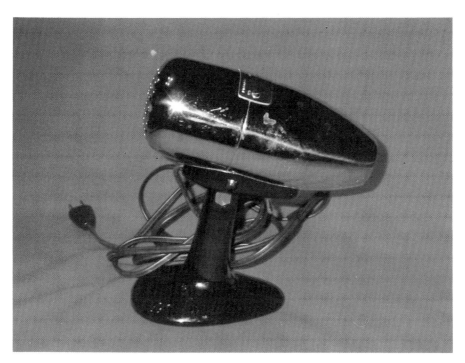

"Oyster Air Jet" hair dryer. Black Bakelite stand. $25-34.

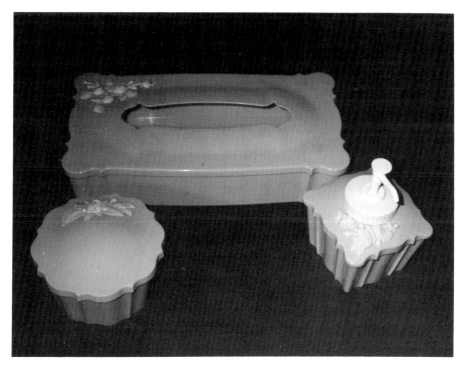

Three piece dresser set marked "Schwarz Bros. Plastics." $15-20.

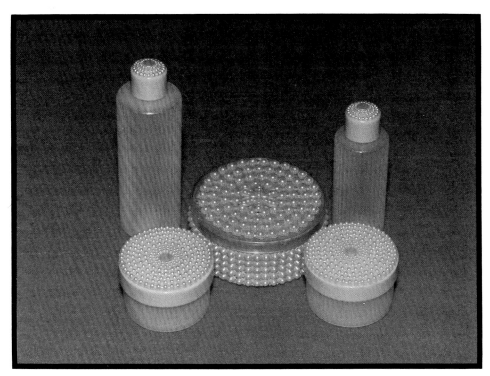

Five-piece dresser set. Pink plastic, $25-35.

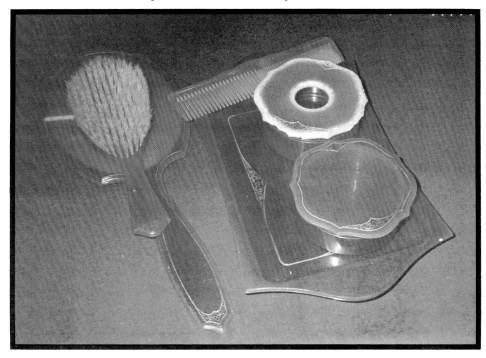

Eight piece dresser set. Celluloid, $35-45.

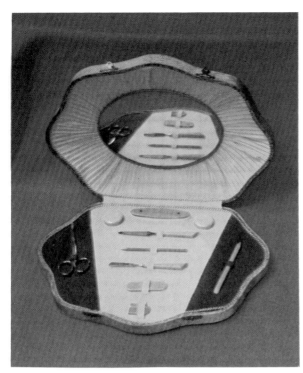

Ten piece dresser set in a velour box. Bakelite handles, $35-45.

Ladies travel set (two pieces missing). Celluloid, $60-75.

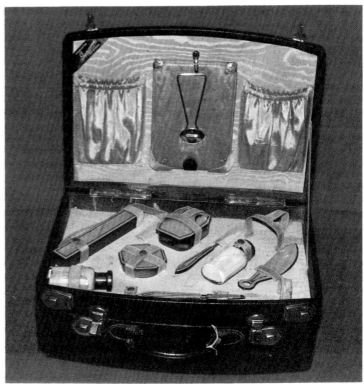

Nine piece dresser set. Green celluloid, $40-50.

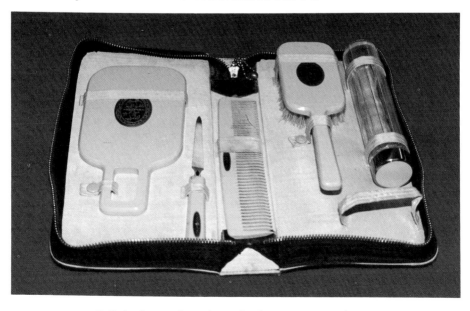

Celluloid travel set (powder box missing), $35-40.

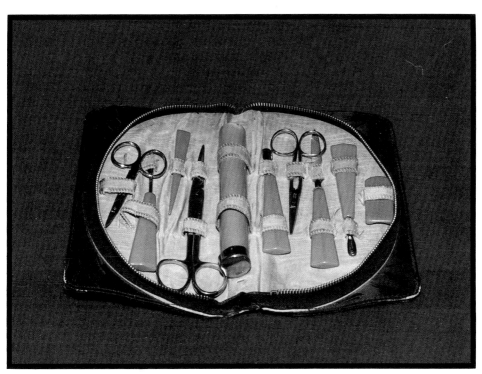

Ten piece manicure set. Celluloid, $45-60.

Celluloid travel set marked "Duraloid Fittings, U.S.A." $35-40.

Powder box marked "Lucite By Dupont." Aqua, $15-20.

Powder box marked "Ciera." Frosted plastic, $15-20.

Jewelry box. Aqua Bakelite, $20-30.

Ivory colored dresser box in an Oriental style. Plastic, $18-22.

Paper weights. Red roses inside Lucite, $25-35 each.

Lucite lipstick holders. Front: triple,$18-22; rear: $22-28.

Lucite perfume bottles, $35-45 each.

Lucite lipstick holders. $20-26 each.

Black child brush. Wood body, plastic brush, $35-40.

Black lady brush. Wood body, plastic brush, $35-40.

Soap dish. Green speckled celluloid, $8-10.

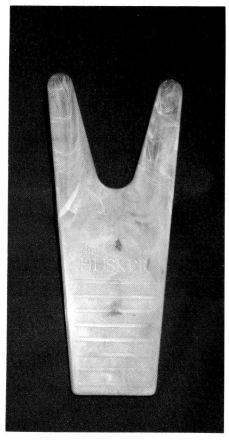

"The Husker" boot jack. Yellow plastic, $12-16.

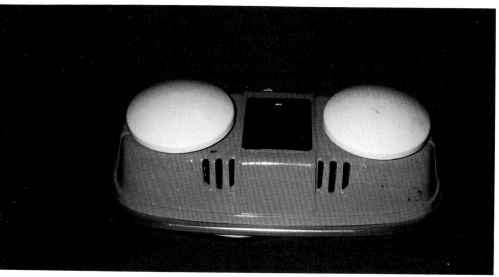

Foot massager marked "Standard Twin DeLuxe, Whittman, Mass." Aqua plastic, $28-35.

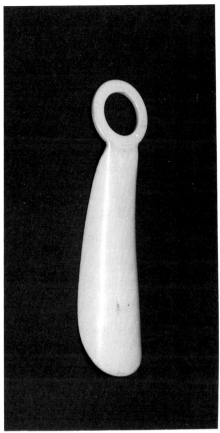

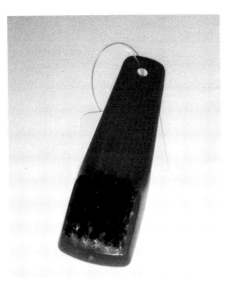

Shoe brush advertising "Hush Puppies." Red plastic, $5-6.50.

Shoe horn. Cream colored celluloid, $4-6.

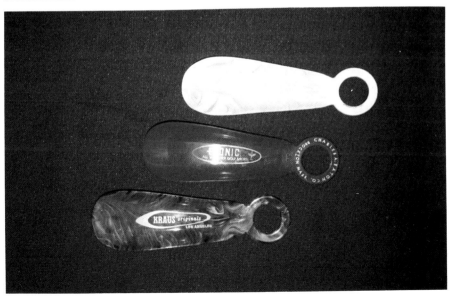

Advertising shoe horns. Yellow, red, and brown plastic, $6-8.

Plant Care

Pink planters with black plastic holders. $6-8.

White planter with a metal stand and plastic bowl, 2' high. $15-22.

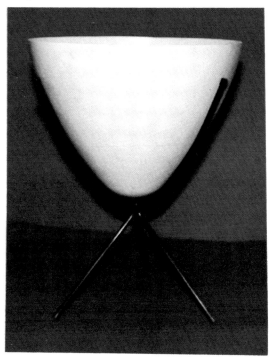

Plant squirter with a glass jar and plastic top, unmarked. $9-12.

Radios and Phonographs

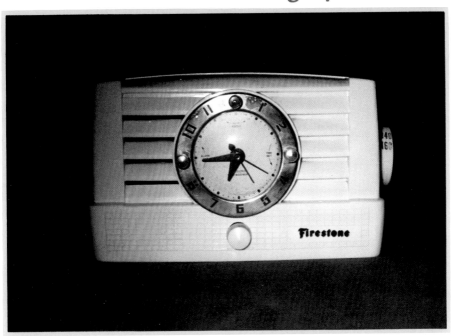

"Firestone" radio. White plastic, $65-75.

"CBS" radio. Green plastic, $50-175.

"Airline" radio. Red plastic, $40-60.

"Motorola" radio. Aqua plastic, $60-125.

"General Electric" radio. Pink plastic. $70-120.

"Crosley" radio. Blue Bakelite, $100-190.

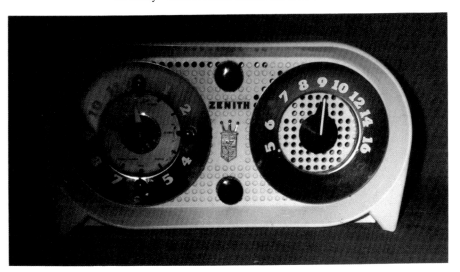

"Zenith" radio. White plastic, $60-175.

"Admiral" radio. Aqua plastic, $60-75.

"General Electric" radio. White Catalin. $125-145.

"True Tone" radio. Brown Bakelite, $100-175.

"Sylvania" radio. Brown Bakelite, $100-160.

"General Electric" radio. Brown Bakelite, $75-125.

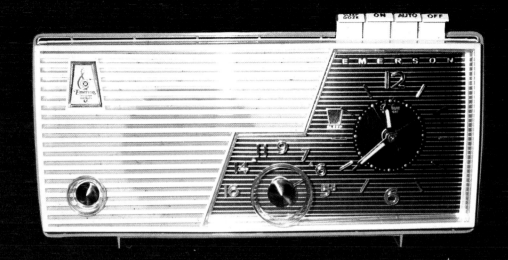

"Emerson" radio. Pink and white plastic, $60-150.

"Zenith" radio. Green Bakelite, $85-125.

"Arvin" radio. White and cream bakelite. $85-100.

"Fada" radio. Cream celluloid. $125-275.

"Crosley" radio. Green Bakelite, $80-250.

"Crosley" radio. Aqua plastic, $85-250.

"Zenith" radios. Aqua and black plastic, $75-125 each.

"Zenith" radio. White Bakelite, $70-125.

"Mickey Mouse" radio. White,$200-350.

"Silvertone" radio. Green plastic, $85-150.

"General Electric" radio. Cream colored plastic, $50-150.

Zenith radio. Brown Bakelite, $50-125.

"General Electric" radio. Red and white plastic, $100-150.

"Emerson" radio. Plastic, $50-150.

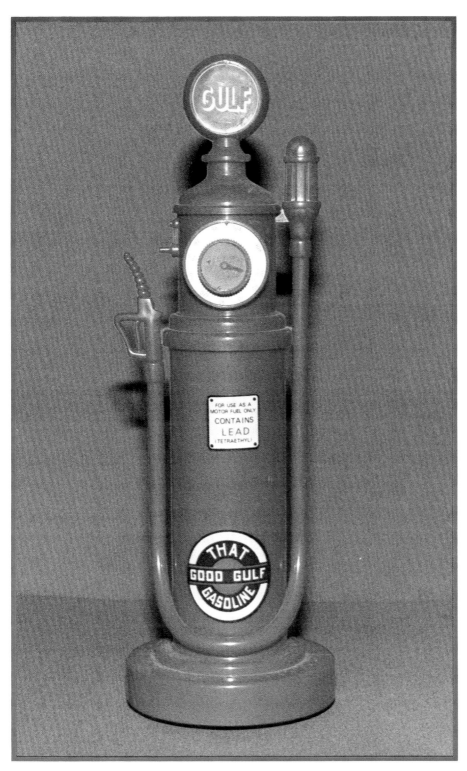

Advertising radio for Gulf Oil. Plastic, $28-35.

"Emerson" phonograph. Brown Bakelite, $45-50.

"Shoo Fly Pie & Apple Pan Dowdy" phonograph record by Vogue. Plastic, $65-75.

"Basin Street Blues" phonograph record by Vogue. Plastic, $60-70.

Recreation

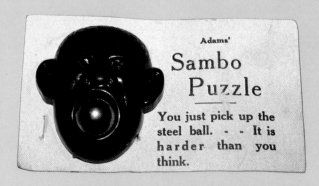

Puzzle marked "Adams Co., Sambo." Plastic, $70-80.

Fish hook. The barrel moves up, revealing that the man is nude. Plastic, $85-100.

Game cube dispenser. Clear with a brown stand. Plastic, $10-13.

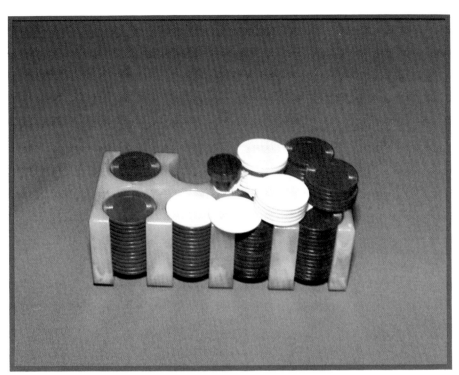

Poker chips and case. Red, white, and blue Catalin, $22-27.

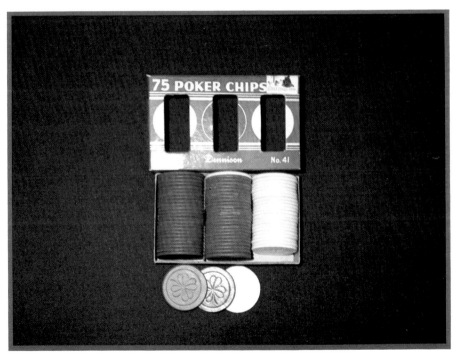

"Dennison" poker chips. Red, blue, and white plastic, $8-10.

Sewing

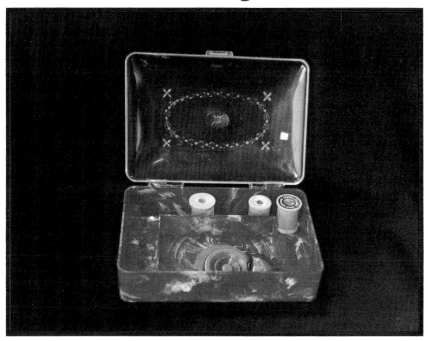

Red pre-war plastic sewing box, $10-14.

Pre-war plastic sewing box with a lid, marked Hommer Mfg.
Co." Red, $9-12.

Sewing box marked "U.S.A. Plastic, $14-18.

Sewing box. Pink plastic, $8-12.

Lady sewing box. Pink plastic, $10-14.

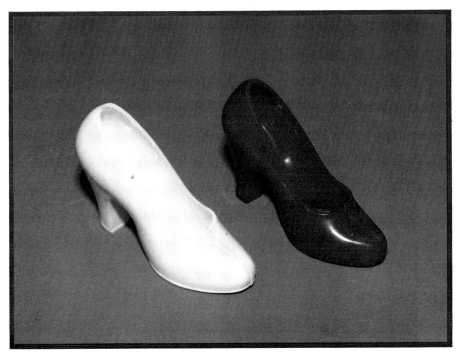

Shoe pin cushions. Red and white plastic, $3-6.

Smoking Accessories

Cigarette pack holder with leather band marked "Fosta Prod. Plastic." $5-8.

Donkey cigarette holder. Plastic, $22-30.

Musical cigarette dispenser. White Bakelite, $40-55.

Ash tray marked "U.S.A." Brown Bakelite, $30-40.

Telephones

Black Bakelite telephone, $165-195.

Black Bakelite telephone, $175-200.

Black and white Bakelite telephone, $150-175.

Black Bakelite telephone, $165-190.

Black Bakelite telephone earpiece, with a brass base. Marked "Strongberg Carlson," $190-225.

Black Bakelite telephone, marked "Signal Corp., U.S. Army," $125-150.

Kid's Stuff

Baby Things

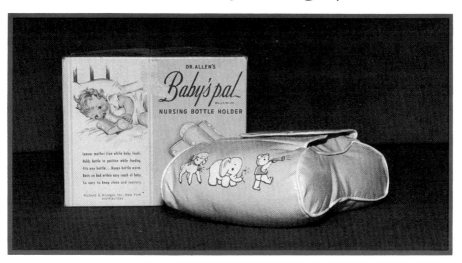

Nursing bottle holder, marked "Richard Krueger Co. N.Y." Pink vinyl, $12-15.

Child's night light. Plastic, $25-30.

Wee Wee Jug by Westland Plastics, California. "A Urinal For Little Squirts." Yellow plastic, $8-12.

Banks

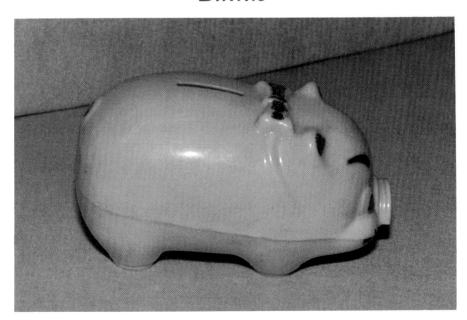

Pink piggy bank, marked "General Art Craft Inc." Plastic, $10-13.

Piggy bank. Yellow plastic, $10-14.

Clear plastic piggy bank, marked "Japan," $8-10.

Red elephant bank, marked "Rexall Drugs, Jumbo Values."
Plastic, $10-14.

Advertising banks. Plastic, $8.50 each.

"Eveready Batteries" bank. Black plastic, $12-15.

Dolls

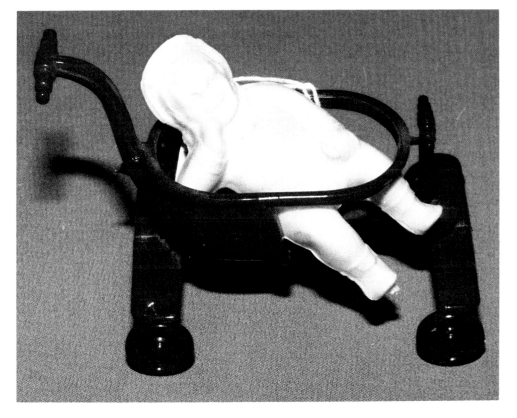

Baby in a stroller child's toy. Red plastic, $6-9.

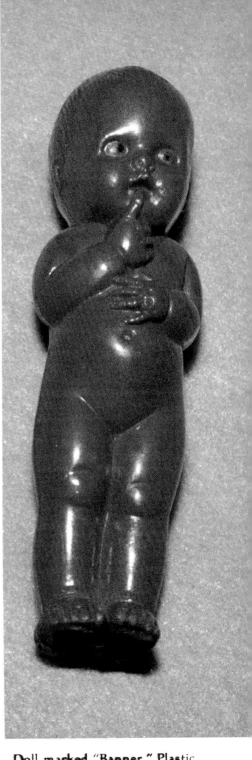

Doll with jointed arms and legs.
marked "Italy." Plastic, $18-25.

Doll marked "Banner." Plastic,
$18-22.

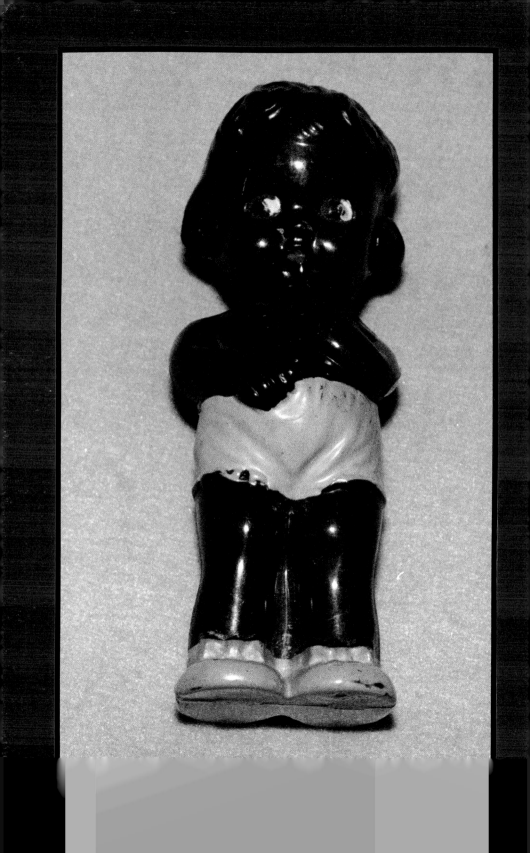

Doll with jointed arms and legs marked "Japan." Celluloid, $25-30.

Baby doll with eyes that open and close, and jointed arms and legs. Marked "Japan." Plastic, $15-20.

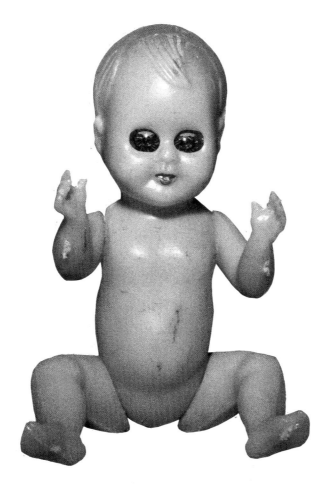

Doll with jointed arms and legs, marked "Japan." Celluloid, $20-26.

Doll with grass skirt, marked "Japan." Plastic, $18-22.

Rattles

Child's rattle. Green turtle shell with celluloid handle, $10-14.

Plastic baby rattles. Dog In Bubble, $7; Uncle Sam, $10; Mallet, $5; Phone, $7.

Bunny baby rattle, marked "Knickerbocker Plastic Co." Yellow, $8-10.

Bunny baby rattle, marked "Knickerbocker Plastic Co." Pink, $6-8.

Chick baby rattle, marked "Knickerbocker Plastic Co." Yellow, $8-10.

Mickey Mouse baby rattle, marked "Davera, Walt Disney." Plastic, $8-10.

Toys

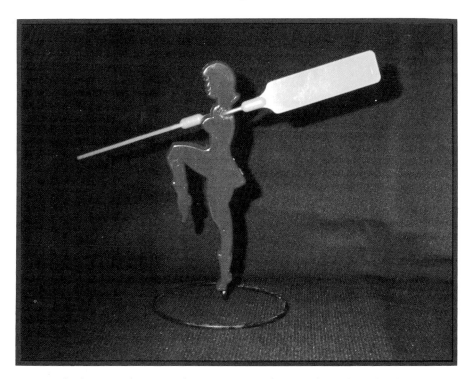

Whirligig with arms that rotate in the wind. Red and yellow plastic, $10-14.

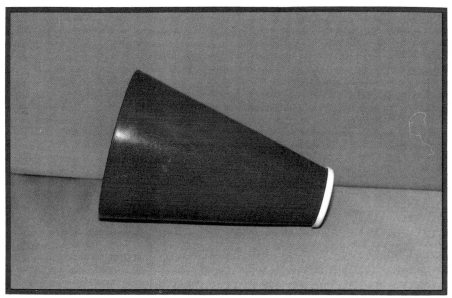

Megaphone marked "U.S.A." Red plastic, $6-9.

Easter Bunny in cart child's toy marked "U.S.A. Plastic Products,"
$12-15.

Child's table ware marked "Joy Toy, Banner, N.Y." Plastic,
$8-12.

Child's dish set in the box. Plastic, $35-40.

Doll furniture, 3 pieces. Marked "Marx Co." Aqua plastic, $15-20.

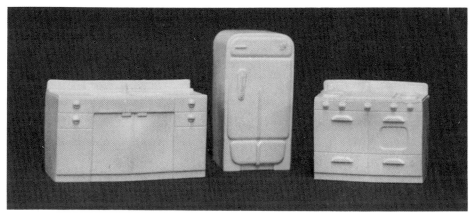

Doll furniture, 3 pieces. Marked "Marx Co." Pink plastic, $15-20.

Doll furniture, 5 pieces. Marked "Marx Co." Pink plastic, $20-25.

How Plastics
Are Made

Plastics come from natural resources that include petroleum, natural gas, coal, water, wood, salt, air, and limestone. These are broken down into carbon, hydrogen, oxygen, and nitrogen atoms, with carbon being the basic component of plastics. The way these elements are combined and treated with heat determines the type of plastic made.

There are two basic ways of creating plastics. In the traditional manner, the raw materials of plastic are changed by the use of heat, pressure, and a catalyst (a substance that causes chemicals to react to each other, but does not itself become part of the final result). The latest technologies avoid the use of heat, pressure, and catalysts by shooting powerful doses of radiation through the raw materials. The results are the same but better control is achieved with this method because the plastic stops changing as soon as the radiation is switched off.

The four principal types of organic plastics are: (1) Synthetic resins; (2) natural resins; (3) cellulose derivatives; and (4) protein substances. A brief description of each of these groups will acquaint the reader to the characteristics of each type.

Synthetic resin plastics—When combined with suitable fillers, these plastics are molded into lightweight products with excellent strength and dimensional stability. They also have resistance to the elements which cause deterioration such as moisture and sunlight. Products are rapidly manufactured in large quantities of accurately sized parts by the application of heat and pressure to the material placed in suitable molds. Casting resin and laminated resinous products are made into sheets, rods, or tubes. Machine operations cut blanks from these for the finished product. Some of the cheap raw materials used in the production of resin plastic include formaldehyde, phthalic anhydride, acetylene, and petroleum. This plastic is commonly known under trade names as Bakelite, Catalin, Beetle, Glyptal, and Vinylite. Resin plastics are used in such things as electrical parts, containers, clothing accessories, including buttons, buckles, jewelry, and miscellaneous novelties.

Natural Resins—The natural resins that are the basis of these plastics are commonly known by such names as shellac, rosin, asphalt, and pitch. They are used in industry for the production of the fusible type of molded product as distinguished from the infusible articles formed by some of the synthetic resins. Hot-molding compositions are prepared by mixing shellac, rosin, and asphalts with suitable fillers. Compositions containing mainly shellac as the binder are used in insulators for high voltage equipment, telephone parts, and phonograph records.

Cellulose Derivatives—This organic plastic is probably the most used and best known of any plastic. Celluloid plastics are used for toys, toilet articles, pen and pencil barrels, camera film, safety glass, windows, and lacquers. The raw material cellulose, is found in fairly pure, fibrous condition as ordinary cotton or pulped wood. Treatment with chemicals converts cellulose into compounds which can be formed into desired shapes. Cellulose plastics excel in toughness and flexibility, conduct heat slowly, and can be made tasteless, odorless, and transparent.

Protein substances—These plastics are named according to the protein source of the material; for example, casein plastic from skimmed milk and soybean meal from soybeans. These protein substances are thoroughly kneaded into a colloidal mass, which is then formed into rods, tubes, and sheets by suitable presses. The formed pieces are then hardened by treatment with formaldehyde. Buttons, buckles, beads and game pieces are made by this process.

The two main groups that plastics fall into are thermoplastics and thermosets. Thermoplastics can be changed into different shapes by pressing or molding them while they are softened by heat. They will keep the new shape when they are cool but when reheated they will soften again and may be reshaped into something quite different. Thermoplastics are made from ethylene, propylene, oil, benzine, chlorine, and salt. Types of thermoplastics include fluorocarbons, cellulosics, polyvinyl chloride, styrenes, vinyls, polypropylene, polyethylene, nylon, and acrylics. Some examples of products they are used for include handbags, ice cube trays, eye glass frames, bowls, doll parts, hair brushes, and golf tees.

Thermosets may also be softened and molded, but only once. After they have been heated they undergo a chemical change so that, when cool and hard, they keep their shape forever and cannot be remolded. The thermosets made of formaldehyde, nitrogen, coal, air, and cellulose sources such as cotton, wood pulp, and corncobs. They include the epoxies, polyesters, aminos, Bakelite, urea, melamine, and phenolics. Some examples of these are bottles, poker chips, makeup cases, knobs, and buttons.

Most chemical names of plastics are complicated and difficult to pronounce. Sometimes the chemical name of the resin is used and in other cases the trade name is used. Some inventors even used "catchy" names. Because of the great variety of terminology and to avoid considerable confusion, the following list of manufacturers and trade names will help the collector identify products. It is impossible to make a complete list because new materials are developed and named each year.

Trade name	Plastic Family	Producer
Abson	Styrene	B.F. Goodrich Co.
Acrylite	Acrylic	American Cyanamid Co.
Alathon	Polyolefins	E.I. DuPont de Nemours Co.
Alkanex	Polyester coating materials	General Electric Co.
Ameripol	Polyethylene	Goodrich-Gulf Chemical Co.
Amester	Polyester resins	American Alkyd Industries
Araldrite	Epoxy	Ciba Products
Armalite	Foamed insulation	Armstrong Cork Co.
Arnel	Cellulose	Celanese Corp. of America
Aropol	Polyester resin	Archer-Daniels-Midland Co.
Atlac	Polyester resin	Atlas Powder Co.
Avisco	Urea-formaldehyde	American Viscose Corp.
Avisun	Polypropylene	Avisun Corp.
Bakelite	Polyolefins, vinyl, styrene, phenolic, epoxy	Union Carbide Co.
Beetle	Urea-formaldehyde	American Cyanamid Co.
Beckosol	Alkyd resins	Reichholh Chemicals, Inc.
Boltaflex	Vinyl sheets	Bolta Products Div. General Tire-Rubber Co.
Boltaron	Styrene	Bolta Products Div. General Tire-Rubber Co.
Celanese	Acetates, polyethylene film, polyester resins	Celanese Corp. of America.
Celcon	Acetal	Celanese Corp. of America.
Chem-o-sol	Vinyl plastics	Chemical Products Corp.
Chevron	Polypropylene	California Chemical Co.
Clopan	Vinyl film	Clopay Corp.
Crest foam	Vinyl foam	Crest Chemical Industries Corp.
Cyclolac	Styrene	Marbon Chemical Co.
Cymac	Styrene	American Cyanamid Co.
Cymel	Melamine	American Cyanamid Co.
Cyzac	Laminating resins	American Cyamanid Co.
Dacron	Polyester fiber	E.I. DuPont de Nemours Co.
Derlin	Acetal	E.I. DuPont de Nemours Co.
Dow Corning	Silicones	Dow Corning Corp.
Durez	Phenolic and Polyester resins	Durez Plastics Div. Hooker Chemical Co.
Dylan	Polyethylene	Koppers Chemical Co.
Dylene	Polystyrene	Koppers Chemical Co.
Dylite	Expandable Polystyrene	Koppers Chemical Co.
Elastofoam	Vinyl plastisol	Union Carbide Plastics Co.
Elrex	Polyolefins and Polystyrene	Rexall Drug Co.
Epilote	Epoxy resin	Shell Chemical Co.
Epiphen	Epoxide resin	Borden Chemical Co.
Epocast	Casting, bonding, laminating resins	Furane Plastic Co.
Epolene	Polyethlene resins	Eastman Chemical Products, Inc.
Epon	Epoxy resins	Shell Chemical Co.
Epotuf	Epoxy resins	Richhold Chemicals, Inc.
Epoxical	Tooling resins	U.S. Gypsum Co.
Escon	Polypropylene	Enjay Chemical Co.
Ethafoam	Polyethylene foam	Dow Chemical Co.
Ethocel	Ethyl Cellulose	Dow Chemical Co.
Evanglo	Polystyrene	Koppers Co., Inc.

Trade name	Plastic Family	Producer
Evr-Kleer	Cast acrylic sheet	Cast Optics Corp.
Fiberite	Reinforced phenolic, melamine, and epoxy molding materials	The Fiberite Corp.
Formica	High pressure laminate	Formica Corp. Subsidiary of American Cyanamid
Forticel	Cellulose propionate	Celanese Corp. of America
Fortiflex	Polyethylene	Celanese Corp. of America
Fortisan	Rayon fiber	Celanese Corp. of America
Fortrel	Polyester fiber	Fiber Industries, Inc.
Fosta Nylon	Nylon	Foster Grant, Inc.
Fosta	Tuf-flex high-impact polystyrene	Foster Grant, Inc.
Fostalite	Light-stable polystyrene	Foster Grant, Inc.
Fostarene	Polystyrene	Foster Grant, Inc.
Genco Acrylic	Cellulose, acetate butyrate, polysthylene, and styrenes	General Plastics, Co.
Geon	Vinyl	B.F. Goodrich Co.
Gerlite	Acrylic sheeting	Gering Plastics
Ger-Pak	Polyethylene film	Gering Plastics
Glykon	Polyester resins	Chemical Div., General Tire and Rubber Co.
Grex	High density polyethylene	W.R. Grace and Co.
Halcon	Fluorocarbon	Allied Chemical Co.
Hetron	Polyester	Durez Plastics Div., Hooker Chemical
Hysol	Epoxy	Hysol Corp.
Implex	Acrylic	Rohm and Haas
Kel-F	Fluorocarbon	Minnesota Mining and Mfg. Co.
Kodapak	Cellulosics	Eastman Kodak Co.
Kodel	Polyester fiber	Tennessee Eastman Co.
Krene	Vinyl	Union Carbide Plastics Co.
Kynar	Fluorocarbon	Pennsalt Chemicals Corp.
Laminac	Polyester	American Cyanamid Co.
Lemac	Polyvinyl acetate	Borden Chemical Co.
Lexan	Polycarbonate	General Electric Co.
Lucite	Acrylic	E.I. DuPont de Nemours Co.
Lumarith	Cellulose acetate	Celanese Corp. of America
Lustran	Styrene	Monsanto Chemical Corp.
Lustrex	Styrene	Monsanto Chemical Corp.
Marafoam	Urethane foam resins	Marblette Corp.
Maraset	Epoxy	Marblette Corp.
Marblette	Phenolic resins	Marblette Corp.
Marco	Polyester	Celanese Corp. of America
Marcothix	Thixotropic polyester resins	Celanese Corp. of America
Marlex	Polyolefins	Marbon Chemical Co.
Marvinol	Vinyl	U.S. Rubber Co.
Merlon	Polycarbonate	Mobay Chemical Co.
Methocel	Methyl cellulose	Dow Chemical Co.
Micarta	High pressure laminate	Westinghouse Electric Co.
Microthene	Polyethylene	U.S. Industrial Chemical Co.
Mirro-Brite	Metallized acetate, butyrate, styrene	Coating Products Co.
Moplene	Polypropylene	Novamont Corp.
Multaron	Polyester resins	Mobay Chemical Co.

Trade name	Plastic Family	Producer
Mylar	Polyester film	E.I. DuPont de Nemours Co.
Opalon	Vinyl chlorine	Monsanto Chemical Co.
Orlon	Acrylic fiber	E.I. DuPont de Nemours Co.
Paraplex	Polyester resins	Rohm and Haas
Pelespan	Expandable polystyrene	Dow Chemical Co.
Penton	Chlorinated polyether	Hercules Powder Co.
Petrothene	Polyethylene	U.S. Industrial Chemical Co.
Plaskon		
Nylon	Nylon	Allied Chemical Corp.
Plenco	Phenolics	Plastics Engineering Co.
Plexiglas	Acrylic	Rohm and Haas
Plio-Tuf	Styrene	Goodyear Tire and Rubber Co.
Pliovic	Vinyl	Goodyear Tire and Rubber Co.
Plyophen	Phenolic	Reichhold Chemicals, Inc.
Polycast	Acrylic sheets	The Polycast Corp.
Polyfilm	Polyester film	Dow Chemical Co.
Polyfoam	Urethane film	General Tire and Rubber Co.
Polylite	Polyester resins	Reichhold Chemicals Inc.
Poly Pro	Polypropylene	Spencer Chemical Co.
Profax	Polypropylene	Hercules Powder Co.
Saran	Vinylidene chloride	Dow Chemical Co.
Scorbord	Expandable polystyrene	Dow Chemical Co.
Seilon	Vinyl, styrene, polyethylene	Seiberling Rubber Co.
Styrofoam	Expandable polystyrene	Dow Chemical Co.
Styron	Polystyrene	Dow Chemical Co.
Teflon	Fluorocarbon	E.I. DuPont de Nemours Co.
Tenite	Cellulosics and polyolefins	Eastman Chemical Products, Corp.
Texin	Urethane	Mobay Chemical Co.
Textolite	High pressure laminate	General Electric Co.
Thermoflow	Reinforced polyester resin	Atlas Powder Co.
Tyrex	Cellulosic monofilament	E.I. DuPont de Nemours Co.
Tyril	Copolymer of styrene and acrylonitrile	Dow Chemical Co.
Ultron	Vinyl	Monsanto Chemical Co.
Uni-crest	Expandable polystyrene	United Cork Co.
Varcum	Phenolic	Reichhold Chemical Co.
Velon	Vinyl	Firestone Plastics Co.
Versamid	Polyamide resins	General Mills, Inc.
Vibrafoam	Cellular urethane sheet	U.S. Rubber Co.
Vibrin	Polyester	U.S. Rubber Co.
Videne	Polyester film	Goodyear Tire and Rubber Co.
Vuepak	Cellulose acetate	Monsanto Chemical Co.
Vygen	Polyvinyl chloride	General Tire and Rubber Co.
Zerlon	Copolymer of acrylic and styrene	Dow Chemical Co.
Zetafin	Polyolefin copolymers	Dow Chemical Co.
Zytel	Nylon	E.I. DuPont de Nemours Co.

Bibliography

Heimann, Erich. *Do It Yourself With Plastics*. Dutton. N.Y.: 1973.

Lambert, Mark. *Spotlight on Plastics*. Rourke Enterprises. Vero Beach, Florida: 1988.

Claude, Smale. *Creative Plastic Techniques*. Van Nostrand Rhinehold. New York: 1973.

Cope, Dwight. *Cope's Plastic Book*. Goodheart-Willcox. Chicago: 1957.

Jambro, Donald. *Manufacturing Process: Plastics*. Prentice Hall. Englewood Cliffs, New Jersey: 1976.

Swanson, Robert. *Plastics Technology*. McKnight & McKnight. Bloomington, Illinois: 1965.

Cherry, Raymond. *General Plastics*. McKnight & McKnight. Bloomington, Illinois: 1967.

Dineen, Jacqueline. *Plastics: The World's Harvest*. Enslow Pub. Hillside, New Jersey: 1988.

Di Noto, Andrea. *Art Plastic-Designed for Living*. Abbeville Press. New York: 1984.

Buehr, Walter. *Plastics-The Man Made Miracle*. William Morrow. New York: 1967

DuBoise, Harry. *Plastics History U.S.A.* Cahners Books. Boston: 1972.

Encyclopedia Americana. Grolier. Danberry, Conn.: 1990.